From the Inside Out

From the Inside Out

Umar Bin Hassan

Grumble Press

Grumble Press

From the Inside Out
Umar Bin Hassan

Copyright © 2020

Grumble Press
Los Angeles, California

No part of this book may be reproduced without permission of the author and publisher.

Cover art: Sean Mulkey
Editors: Ed Mabrey and Eduardo Vega

ISBN 978-0-578-80260-2

First Edition

Set in My Underwood font, designed by Michael Tension

For every voice silenced, for every ear closed, for every eye shut against its will

Foreword

I formed this press for moments like this—to ensure that Black voices are catalogued and saved in a space that is safe for them. I have known Umar for quite some time now and was shocked to discover he'd never released a book of his own work.

His work isn't something I wanted someone to discover years from now while rummaging through an old shoebox or dresser. His work is Black work, meaning the writing of important moments in history by a Black person. Links in a chain, pathways, roots of a tree, pick your comparison but the works of The Last Poets and Umar Bin Hassan are a crucial and critical part of American and Black literature. From Paul Lawrence Dunbar to Kendrick Lamar, you can touch one era and the other with Umar's work firmly between those two points.

At a later date this foreword will no doubt be pages and pages in itself, full of detailed breakdowns and discussions on the true impact Umar's work has had on this planet. But for now I wanted everyone to simply dive into this book and digest his work

Umar is a poet that needs to be heard live

to fully appreciate. We did our best to marry the page's demands with the stage's desires. When Umar first sent me the manuscript it was in pieces and pages, as in actual mailed-to-me pages from a typewriter or scanned copies from a typed-up page. We decided the best way to do the poems justice was to recreate that feeling as best we could in terms of font, layout, and design.

From the Inside Out is the only collection of Umar Bin Hassan's work. We hope you enjoy the poems for generations to come.

Until that day,

Ed Mabrey
Grumble Press

Contents

Whitegirls	14
Trapped	18
Kuumba	20
A Midwestern Poem for a Midwestern Prince	23
Trane-Cepts	26
This Is Madness!	30
The Illusion of Self	32
Shoeshine Boy	35
Personal Things	40
Silence of the Jams	43
Brainstorms. Rainstorms. Painstorms.	45
New Orleans	47
Flowing	48
Rhytmagic	50
Wilt	52
Asian Winds	54
Sonny	56
The Queen Mothers	59

Kings of Pain	64
Young Love	67
MEN-tality	69
Jimi Ju Ju	72
Homesick	76
Sort It Out	80
25 Years	83
Monument	86
HOLLOW WOOD	87
Grace	89
Sacred to the Pain	91
Love	93
Power	96

Whitegirls

That last bit of shame
has finally followed
her violator
out of the room

Her eyes are
glazed and focused
on the ceiling
There will always
be those ceilings

She rises up
and begins
to let go
She will
learn how
to let go
at a **very**
young age

She begins to run

She runs away

She runs
from herself
She runs
games
She runs
tricks
She runs
for that Higher
Office in her mind

Porn stars
Torn stars
Born stars
clicking their magic
slippers beside the
casting couch and
a dream stuck
somewhere between
poor white trash
and rich white
privilege
becomes her
credibility and
then her
disability
in finding
her own voice

Her own time

Her own resolve

And sometimes
without warning
and without
reason her emotions
begin to affect
her directly and
indirectly

You can feel
the sexual
intensity
in her work
in her auditions
in her High School
cheers are the most precise

the most exact
the most possessed

Her flirtations
with the Friday night
crowd seem so innocent
and yet so very
obvious She must be
noticed She must be
affirmed Her struggles
with rejection
are so passionate
so driven
so driven
Whitegirls
hold secrets
and they hold
them very well

They hold them
to the point
where only time
will tell

Swept-up hairdos either
more or less
The soul is in torment
but refuses to confess
She hits the streets
locked and loaded
strolling and rolling
like the outlaw
she has become

She comes into the
realization that she
goes very well with

the soft warm tones
of Miles Slow and easy
tokes of the powder
Elegant and refreshing
sips of champagne

Players
bring the game
She brings the facts
Yes she can play naive
Yes she can play easy
And yes she can give
as good as she gets
Languishing lamenting
lucid longing
lustful loyal
legitimate leaning
and lively lesbian arts
and crafts of conceiving
and believing in her
own happy endings

So what do you want from her
What do you need from her
Long blonde hair
blowing in the wind
of convertible ease
Do you want it soft
fragile and tied down
Or do you want it
Strong dominant on top
and untouchable

Whitegirls know how
to play roles
and play them very well

Trapped

The children on the corners, in the jails, in the wind. What spider is this who spins a web of baubles and bangles. Are we trapped? Will we forever stay entwined? Throwing benjamins up into the air when you should be on the ground searching for gold. Finding comfort and sanctuary in Master Charge, Visa, debt and illusion. One last cheer for the almighty dollar.

Dark clouds on the horizon. Understanding is being dashed against the rocks. The ripples of the sea are bringing forth blood. Common decency and respect have settled in for the winter, playing with one another in the kiddie corner. Laughing and giggling at each adolescent touch.

Unknown poets seek our ears. Calling out to us from deep and unmarked graves. When will we stop and wonder why? Have we all become mannequins standing limp in the face of truth? Big City lights losing us amongst the asphalt lies and candy cotton swirl of carnival minds. Whew. Whew. Even the Wind is trying to tell us to seek higher ground

The children on the corners, in the jails, in the wind. Why are there so many reflections of loneliness when there are supposed to be people around me? Their tears are out of control. They are flooding my vision of tomorrow. Bombs dropping constantly in other countries. Unborn babies dying in carefully planned cremations.

Time and time again we are being harassed by spastic heroes. Heroes who speak maggots for words. Heroes who vomit in the eyes of sabbath. Heroes who unleash killer locusts upon our dignity. Run. Run. The ocean is going to sail without us. The stars have no sympathy of our allegiance with darkness. The birds are not singing, they are not winging, and we can't fly.

Grounded with the sinister burden of free enterprise, the bling bling and SUVs and soaring gas prices and high crime areas and low esteem and mags murder and insults upon our intelligence and MTV Cribs and political corruption and the children on the corners, in the jails, in the wind, what spider is this who spins a web of baubles and bangles. Are we trapped? Will we forever stay entwined?

Kuumba

She is the Jaliyaa. She did not leave us to die
in the burning and ransacked villages. She did not
leave our souls to rot in the bellies of sharks. She
picked us up and out of the bile and vomit and the
blood of our prayers streaming profusely down the
sides of our faith. She landed us gently on our new
beginning while clothing our nakedness in the shadows
of her smile. She was our death
and resurrection. Jesus began a strange and
difficult existence in the crack of the whip
in the rage of the overseer in the lashes
shredding and cutting into his Virgin birth.

The primitive and crudely crafted drums throbbing and pulsating, and contradictions dancing, and she is chanting whose children are these? Moving and feeling through the high register and subtle words of New Orleans. And the Red. And the Green. And the Yellow bandanas flowing and strolling high in the wind. Some called it Spanish. Some called it Creole. Some called it French. She called out Bamboula! Calinda! Ju Jun! The ring shout. The circle dance. A free day. Some free time to call on our science. To call on our Mathematics. To construct our cipher to genius. To self-image. To memories.

Moving in and out of this counterclockwise motion swaying in Rhythm. Feet stomping the earth. Swaying in Time. Feet stomping the EARTH answers back in the voices of our choirs. Our churches. Our gospel is where she baptized us in the harmony, in the melody of field songs, work songs, and secret songs of the Mississippi Delta and the BLUES striking a familiar chord in the clickety clack, clickety clack, of the train wheels moving us up north to Memphis and the honkytonks. To Kansas and the boogie woogie. To St. Louis and the rag time. And to Chicago and the funky sound of our circular breathing that taught us how to swing and to sing in the scat of jazz and the razz matazz of be bop and the developing magic of hip hop. And the Blood of Biggie. And the Tears of Tupac forever resting in her sound. She is our music. She is our dance. She is our art. She is our freedom. She is Kuuumba.

A Midwestern Poem for a Midwestern Prince

Trudging thru deep deep snow and blizzard like winds smashing up against your face. Trying to get to somewhere anywhere soon. The sounds and rhythms of the machines in the factories booming out their concertos to our receptive ears. We walked with that and we talked with that. It was our swing and then our bop. The way we hipped and the way we hopped.

Our clothes our style. That Motown wile. Those Midwestern challenges. That Midwestern funk. Brothers and sisters huddled together. That burden of anticipation. Your mother. My mother. Cowering behind fractured moments and the illusion that blind devotion could solve the unsolvable.

Genius struggling against the brilliance of itself. My father. Your father. Musicians. Talented creative productive and highly frustrated by the dead ends and dead stops that impeded and curtailed their progression. The future looking for someone to take it forward. You took up that mantle and I took up that mantle and we never ever forgot where we came from.

A soft kiss of wine emboldens the passion. A dimmed red light eases the apprehension and doubt. The Delfonics make their presence known. The heat of the moment is so right up against the wall under the stairs in between the washer and dryer where it all becomes so juicy and wet. A promise. A proposition. A phenomenon when those basements started to grind. Those Midwestern challenges.

That Midwestern funk. That church piano, why don't you call me anymore? You could be church Prince. That Sunday morning solo. That voice that could bring the congregation to the best of themselves. You could be that doo wop singer on the corner holding and preserving the highest note of our pleasures and fantasies. Was Warner Music a challenge? No, just a matter of time. Was Purple Rain a challenge? No, just your poetic rhyme was all. The music you created a challenge? No, just the essence of your sublime. The 2007 Alma Awards. Sheila E coming down the aisle. Prince already at the altar. This night. This time. This union will become a force. A direct assault upon our senses. The audience had better check their immune systems. They could catch cold, because it's about to become very very cool up in here. That soaring guitar. Those scorching timbales. Si Mami. Si Papi. You Brother. You Sister. We can do this. We are this. That High Order of Afro Cuban, African American musical collaborations.

Thank you Dizzy. Thank you Chano. A marvelous rendition of call and response. The merengue. The salsa. That piano. The horns giving a shout out to their cousins of the blues the jazz and the funk of the dancers on stage giving credence to who we are and where we came from. Music is the sound of beauty and you displayed and dispensed that beauty as well as anybody, Prince. A new symbol for your fans. Avid followers. Deeply devoted believers in your talent and humanity. Wherever you were was where they wanted to be. By bus by car by train by plane. You mesmerized, you tantalized, you romanticized them with death-defying acts of musical genius.

The speed, velocity, and depth of your splits and turns, the acrobatic joyous atmosphere you brung to every corner of the stage. You were that whirling dervish that baptized us in the name of feeling good about ourselves while being at ease in the presence of others. You had that magic of transforming adults into gleeful little children. And we were okay with that. We could handle that, because we could feel the love and respect you were sharing with us as we were sharing it with you. You made us feel like family. The human family. The women in your life loved you, trusted you. They allowed you to explore their passions their doubts their moments of joy.

Every moment that you were accepted into their presence you always tried to make them feel big about themselves. They adored that they cherished that because they knew that as long as you were trying to love and accept them that you would truly learn how to love yourself. Sleep well brave Prince, for your deed and proclamations shall be forever renowned throughout the land. I pledge to you that with all my heart and words I will try to make sure that no purple rain ever gets stuck in the clouds again.

Trane-Cepts

Om Om Om   Ala Bama   Kulu Se Mama Kule Se Mama   Ala Bama Ala-Bama   And this is for Love And this is for Peace   My Favorite Things   My Favorite Things   Om   Om   Om   A ceremonial priest. He liberated the oment at hand. He was not an exaggeration. There was no lack of confidence here.

He instinctively went after the nuances before they got to him. The horn was celebrated. The sequences in between the interludes. He managed the energy so well. How did he do it? Where did it come from? Saxophone slashing through the pretense of this obscurity. Why does the melody linger go long? Were we part of this sound somewhere someplace long time ago?

Why is it so familiar? Alone with these thoughts but nowhere to land. Holding air over crowded dreams and a distant fog. Speaking in the youth of good old days, and yet, someone forgot to tell me that this gig could be over very soon. Silver cycles of layers of chords and notes becoming pleasant smiles and velvet promises. Down home blues dressed in uptown coolness. Respectfully closing my eyes to this very holy undressing of sound.

Trane played for lovers in the ragged nights of their caustic dominions   where the Body and Soul become one in the shattered glass and jagged openings. Where the body and soul become one in the lingering doubts of our Fathers   our Sons   our Holy Ghosts The clashing   The dashing   The smashing of chains pains   and the remains   of love, respect and consideration for their existence as well as his.

A magnificent and moving portrait of brotherhood and unity. Dance with Fat Girl Jimmy. Give her a whirl. Give her a twirl. Give that girl some love and watch her work. Run those hands all up and down and over her body. Her lips Her breasts Those inner thighs Touch Fat Girl Jimmy like soft sunrise rhythms leaving their touch upon the awakening of dawn. Dance with Fat Girl Jimmy. Dance.

The base The base covers the ground securing the perimeters. Closing in on our boredom. Subtle Charming Elusive That Tinkle That Tinkle Of Joplin Of Waller Of Monk all wrapped up in their influence All consumed by their pianos gliding gliding back and forth looking for a way out to find a way in. That tinkle tinkle of McCoy finding himself in the midst of circumstance seeking out different venues with new and bold geographics to travel. Suggesting somewhat extreme, difficult, and yet wonderful possibilities. The piano sounding very good and very necessary at this particular time.

That Tinkle That Tinkle falling falling like gentle leaves upon our wounds Here comes Elvin! Here comes Elvin Jones! Here comes that Midwestern player bringing all that Midwestern noise All that Midwestern Funk! Elvin Jones! The one and only true original beatbox. Round and round he goes and where he stops nobody knows. Hit Trane from the top Elvin hit him from the top. Left hand Right foot. Right hand Left foot. The cymbal.

The base bottom. The who do the voodoo that you do so well Elvin Push up on him. Challenge him. Challenge him with those counter-rhythms Those polyrhythms The drums The drums The power behind the throne. Throwing gasoline on the fire.

Exercising our futility while easing in and out of heavy conversations. The improvisations of inclinations. The major shifts of minor riffs Jimmy. McCoy. Elvin all Chasin The Trane to the light at the end of the tunnel. Will somebody please wake up Bach and tell him that there is some real music going on here. I heard you that morning Trane. I heard you that morning inside the harmony.

I heard the ocean run to kiss the shore as the sun exposed itself from the bowels of your horn. And the saxophone became a voice of time reached out to transform you into a spiritual breath that no man or woman could deny. Trane is Cookin! Trane is Cookin! Scream Trane. Scream past papier-mâché whores turning them into silken beauties. Scream Trane Scream past bleeding and open lacerations going unseen by the human eye. Scream Trane scream past nodding afterthoughts turning them into soprano sweetness fills the air. Take us away from here Trane Take us Away Away Away

This sound of sanctuary becomes a place where all can rest and reside. Why must we pretend? In moments like these in the event of fear and insecurity would you please leave the room and close the door behind you. A moment in time when times becomes so sensitive. And it goes on and on and on this fusion of dreams and paradise of a Love Supreme A Love Supreme. . . Feel the heat. Feel the warmth. Bathe in the intensity of love all around.

Into the journey. Into the exodus. Into the understanding of leaving self-destructive thoughts behind. The meditations. The incantations. The salutations. Touching   Feeling   Sharing   Inspiring our deeds to be this kind.   The First Trane   The Soul Trane   The Blue Trane   And the Last Trane   Giving a quote. Something controlled. Something remote   om   om   om.

This Is Madness!

All my dreams have been turned into psychedelic nightmares with Rosemary's baby pissing in my face and Tiny Tim sticking his moldy penis into my bleeding mind as it cries for the strength to repel the sanctimonious sounds of the white rock group the Grateful

Dead! are my aspirations as they struggle for a free sweet smelling breath of life while being choked by the Christianic gas passed by the Most Reverend Bishop J. Fulton Sheen as he socks it to us in the name of the Lord now.

And my realities have turned into a stone figuration of Miss Liberty as she stands on the corners of the world selling herself to anyone with the head of George Washington on them. And all the while he sits on a throne of Eagle shit with DDT in one hand and a white tornado in the other wearing a crown of castrated Black dicks while reading the non-violent thoughts of Ghandi.

And I watch him relax by playing golf with Roy Wilkins balls with Bayard Rustin glued to his thang while xerox copies of Martin Luther King, Jr. are popping from his skull. To dream the impossible dream. Knock! Knock! Who's there? It's Rap Brown and if you don't open up I'll strike and light and burn your house down.

I see Malcolm's spirit, its eyes burning red black and green flames and crying tears of Thunderbird wine that seem to touch my lips and make me become thirsty for a taste of freedom!

Freedom by any means necessary. It's necessary to have freedom by any means necessary. And I begin to hate with love and love with hate. This is madness! This is madness! This is madness! And 1 look up and see the moon bleeding lifeless white maggots and screaming for my help as the eagle's claws rip and tear at its virginal form. Oh Isis. Oh Tuthmosis. Oh Sun Ra. Oh Allah. Bismillahi Nir Raheem give me your undying strength to rise up and reorder. We're born under the sign Taurus the Bull because all we do is bullshit!

This is madness. This madness is madness. All this madness is madness. Madness this is. Please stop all this madness! Please stop all this madness! Please stop all this madness. Stop.

                Madness!   Madness!   Madness!
madness....
              Madness!   madness....
                                            madness....
  Madness!   madness....
            madness....
madness....   Madness!
             Madness!
Madness!
      madness....   madness....
    madness....   ....STOP!
          Madness!
Madness!   madness....
   madness....

The Illusion of Self

The holy terror becomes the holy blessing. Family values caught in the act of undressing. Addicts getting high in early morning hours. Running through dreams and trampling down flowers. Dancing fast to keep from crying. Inflicting pain to keep from lying. Muggers, B Boys, and heavy metal. Trolls under the bridge in Hansel and Gretel. Pornography, rape and child abuse. Mass murderers quoting Dr. Seuss. Black becomes white with its own illusion.

Money becomes God to complete the confusion. Daily visits to late night clubs. Disappointment, frustration, and ticket stubs. Sad little men in sad little rooms. Sad little openings become sad little tombs. Silent storms and baby screams. Wide open spaces of unconscious streams. The churches are empty, the choirs are full. He takes a snort, she takes a pull.

The sun was dim that childish morning when sleep awakened me to the cries of your distant touch. There were no crowded rooms for our love to cross. No smoke-filled fantasies to insure our happiness. Ours had become a comedy of errors A tragedy from the dark side of the moon. Conversations had become shrieks and shrills in the echoes of laughter. But still we tried. Two muted poets cemented together by the glamour of ticker tape parades. Birds flying free in the torment of our slavery. Had our love become a saga of jagged peaks and stagnant dreams.
Two addicted lovers strung out in the heavens of past romance. Walks in the park could not even

soothe the savageness of tomorrow's presence. Had we become petrified artists who could only paint terrified portraits of love? Had we lost inspiration in the park and slimy swamp of some foreign smile. We could not wait on the rest of the world to comprehend. We could not wait on gracious slaves to snatch their freedom from the havens of gloom. We could not wait on luxurious and pompous expressions to share their feelings with God!

Shirt ties and very well-groomed patronizing that which once was assumed. Round and round the merry go round. Grabbing the ring while stuck to the ground. Little ambitions with great big drugs. Overnight sensations on bearskin rugs. Highly mediocre becomes highly paid. Highly empowered and then highly afraid. Winning becomes everything or nothing at all. Losing your footing and starting to fall.

Women in anger. Women in style. Women dying coming down the aisle. To know how dangerous games can be, to get stuck in a vision but never see. Mistaking pleasure for something to keep taking yourself to be something so deep! Big time lawyers become petty little thieves. Pleading insanity while justice grieves. Pretentious smiles strolling the beach. Life becomes miserable and then out of reach. Subway rides become subway grief. Public transportation becomes a subway thief.

Ours was a moment so divine and yet so very unholy. All around us danced morning prayers giving praises to the lord of the universe while we became atheistic to the thought of giving love to one another. It was raining that morning inside our fears as we cuddled so closely together in the silence of our screams. And you cried. And you cried. When sensitivity found you stranded in the loneliness of windswept waves.

While I caroused with madness in the shadows of my pride. But the smashed and battered face of time kept trying to tell me there is no glory in deceit. Then I did not understand. Now I do. If I could have just one more chance with illusion maybe I could make it real. If I could just take the leftover screams and compose and compose whispering sighs of change. Maybe then you would smile. If I could just take the mystery of night and read it to you from an impromptu poem maybe then then your arms would open in pardon.

Oh yesterday I sorry. Yesterday are you there? Yesterday where are you? And you turn to answer my call. But your eyes. Ooooh your eyes are filled with coffins. The stale sound of funeral trumpets fall from your lips. And I run. And I turn away to question time. But it replies too late. You're both dead! Children in fear, always living inside. Who come out to play only to hide. Their tears are helpless as they fall from the eye. They hit the ground running while trying to fly.

The madness becomes casual at its very best. The mind becomes stronger with every test. They laugh, they smile, they even joke. The challenge to be human at every stroke. Paranoia becomes rumor and then the fear. Intelligence becomes sensitivity and then a tear. Just be who you are and leave it alone. Let them have theirs and you get your own. Rational mind be quiet, ego be still. Learn to accept, learn to be real. To become fully conscious, fully aware. Always loving becomes always fair. To touch, the feel, the sight, the sound. The oneness of you and everything around.

Negative comes and negative goes. Everything changes as the consciousness flows. Always learning, always teaching. Always caring, always reaching. Stick to your path when the going gets rough. Never quitting is never enough. The subtle places inside the mind. The courage to lose. The courage to find. The eagle flying high with the peaceful dove. Always us loving love!

Shoeshine Boy

I.
A homeless man confronts a crucifix he begins to shadow box with it painfully and ferociously throwing punches at its presence.

He so desperately wants to be loved and part of the future. A twisted and tragic political quagmire.

A very substantial and dangerous representation of a satirical cartoon.

The Mother Mary tries to calm his spirit, he spits at her.

A room full of dead stuffed animals and the few sordid remains of an indigenous people has swollen
his chest with pride. Come home. Love is waiting on you.

There is no more glamour in the lights. The money has turned into denial and points of no return. Sad and pathetic has become a crutch.

Are you lost in it?

Consumed by it?

History will record that there will be no victories here, no deaths. Only well-sustained and well-managed misery. Romance, class, and style are so very much needed at this time.

In some slight moment of cognac grace and the warm soft presence of country silence, the speed reaches 135 mph.

I have never false-started at the thought of running the curve, the dynamics have always been in my mind. I have gauged the distance with my soul standing in the windows

of three-year-old day dreams cringing from the fear of mayhem and chaos calling out my name. Arms pumping knees high. I glide into the motion, into the rhythm, into the straightaway

into the razor sharp wind slashing at my face. Welcome to the Midwest where Southern traditions become Northern game. The bitter and biting cold begins to wear my soul like latex gloves.

Standing in the memory of yesterday's childhood procrastination makes one last stand against my mission.

I look back to the projects. They don't answer. My mind begins to make confused and wandering steps toward a destination, any destination.

At that moment stark and desolate eyes peek out from behind closed minds as that first glimpse of death stamps a number upon my back. The voice of defiance becomes my strongest voice. I defy.

All odds, all pain all authority. I even begin to defy the goodness that comes from within myself. The streets become my haven. My sanctuary. My place of worship. Who is God?

What are prayers?

Obsessed and possessed by the religion of human nature. I act and react only to the pain that is bleeding into my future. Feed your family shoeshine boy. Feed your family. Shoeshine. Shoeshine. Can't be beat. Shoeshine.

Shoeshine.

Give your soul a treat.

The great metropolis in front. The tailwinds at my back. In between the moon and Motown I stroll unconsciously thru the arena of misfortune and preserved dreams.

The orange setting of the sun has left me jinns and demons to play. They follow me thru the streets and into the bars. Thru the streets and into the bars.

Thru the streets and into cross body blocks, bull in the ring and quick pitches to the right fading and faking my way thru the crowds, thru the cheers, thru the goal lines of adolescent rebellions on the deep end of deep thoughts

Of Charlie Parker solos in the vast wilderness flashing lights and tortured souls of Benny Rivers. Pierre and Andre's.

The Green Turtle Cafe. The 41 Club. The High Hat. The Tropicana. The Cosmopolitan. Joy's Lounge. And Roxy's. Roxy's. Everybody's juke joint. Roxy's everybody's bucket of Blood. Roxxxy's everybody's dreams and fears.

Ducking under tables while stabbing and shooting at the first thought of being too close to the lies and pretense of being so glad and happy to be up north. Dance shoeshine boy.

Dance. Dance with your laughter. Dance with your joy. Dance with your life. Dance in the streets on the top of bars. Dance for those nickels and dimes. Dance for the women shoeshine boy. They love to see you dance. The Barmaids. The ladies of the evening and sips of Johnny Walker Red from the cleavage of taut and succulent breasts. Dance to all that jazz playing in their eyes to the Miracles and Temptations between their thighs.

To the musty smell of pubic hairs being pressed against your face. And the pervasive lust of wanton and touches of raging clitoris and dripping vulva overwhelm your youthful logic. Your youthful morals. Your youthful reason begins to finger this moment like Jesus walking the water. So Holy. So Fragile. So Temporary.

Dance shoeshine boy. Dance. Shoeshine. Shoeshine. Can't be beat. Shoeshine. Shoeshine. Give your soul a treat.

II.
Point. Madness is the highest form of sensitivity. Counterpoint. I have felt the power and sadness of lulling and stroking dark alleys and dangerous streets to sleep. I have worshipped at the base of the flames.

I have ridden the high secrets of the wind. This will be my last poem about hocus pocus, demons, and the great divide. Sitting here in the midst of God's depression, all these terrified and lonely people trying to tell me jokes. Trying to define my success by the whims of their sanity arouses my suspicion of white picket fences well-structured.

And well-preserved rote learning and honorary degrees that has given way to an acquired sadness that solicits and patronizes a lingering mental disease.

That slight suburban smile has come to reside in a place somewhere between a simple suicide and a synchronized mass murder. The devil decides to join the party. God does not appreciate this moment. He begins to knock out all the lights in the basement.

Somebody is about to get fucked up here. The devil, God, and the shoeshine boy all in the same place at the same time.

Write shoeshine boy. Write The devil refuses to rest on his laurels. He has become number one with a bullet. Choosing his words carefully he makes a thinking man's decision.

He grabs his penis and sticks in a cartridge releasing the safety on the words that are no longer inside his head. They are real now. They take command now. They salute now. He has in fact become a precise military parade that is dazed and confused. The drill cadence.

Personal Things

Time in becomes time out. Group anxieties become personal doubt. Expressing ourselves in dots dots and dashes. Pure cocaine and false eyelashes. Living inside words that seem to lie. Living inside excuses that pass us by. Living inside loneliness becomes a high. Living gets mixed up with wanting to die.

A daily question of going insane while tormenting one another trying to ease the strain. Dreaming of tomorrows we'd like to know. Repressing our thoughts while trying to grow. The heart and soul are not involved. Idle chatter becomes reality while problems go unsolved. Prearranged, prefabricated, and preconditioned.

We're baptized, advertised, and posthumously mentioned. Weaned and groomed for the glory of applause. Living off the mercy of unwritten laws. Shell-shocked patrons making peace with God, while admiring the acrobatics Of a junky's nod. Turned into robots through the power of suggestion. We seek an answer and become the question. Afraid we might die before we live. Blessed with life but then afraid to give.

We want to be amorous, glamorous, and larger than life. Our cheap illusions become high-priced strife. Losing ourselves in times of despair. Becoming self-defeatists of unusual flair. We rush toward the beginning that might be the end. We sit in the darkness and try to pretend.

Pointing fingers while our insides bleed. Committing suicide to fulfill a need. Highly intelligent in a very low way. We speak of existing but have nothing to say. We touch religion and make it seem like hell. But then we touch unholy dreams and wish them well

Faith is replaced with apathy and grief. Indifference is made acceptable and then a belief. Our left eyes all glitter while our right are blind. We submit to this madness and hope it is kind. Distraught women seeking compassion while turning tricks in high Roman fashion. Finding love at the expense of losing their cool. Looking for happiness but finding a fool.

Their moments of trust become deceitful charms. One-night stands in strangers' arms. Carousing with disaster in very high places while cutting off noses to spite their faces. While the men play games of power and glory. Tattered remnants of an old war story. Outside themselves inside their heads, top secret discussions on waterbeds.

Men without neither rhyme nor reason. Lost in the depths of mental treason. Abstract victims of the American dream. Victims of a disguised but well-planned scheme. Victims of a subtle but dangerous game. Rugged individualism with a psychotic name.
We confuse the normal and extort the extreme. We make war a reality and call peace a dream. American contradictions in black and white. We illuminate contradiction and call it the light. America provides you with fortune and fame. While stealing your soul for its own acclaim.

With the English language at its command. It perpetuates illusion throughout the land. Running big games in tiny print, before you've got it, it's already spent. Making sacrificial lambs of the Middle Class. Indulging in rhetoric with its head up it-- lulls you to sleep with the six o'clock news and then wakes you up and spoon-feeds you blues.

But from the darkness of ourselves we can find a brighter day. Understanding and truth must show the way. To understand that everyman's color will not be his heart. To go inside yourself is where it must start. To learn to be considerate. To learn to be humane. To learn to use power and not become vain. To understand you can be strong and not be crude. You can be outspoken and not be rude. To revile the tyrant. To protect the weak. To ensure the innocent their right to be meek. To look on the sea and understand its motion. To understand tenderness and give it devotion. To understand courtesy and to make it a pact, to understand what love is and make it a fact! Because we all must struggle. We all must try. Because somewhere in the future we all must die. But to leave a legacy that will long unfurl. That ours too was a struggle for a better world.

Silence of the Jams

In some lush green moment
of tree top dancing,
Young men with their
visions impaired,
Souls lathered down in
stone,
Blunt instruments softly
caress their minds being
assaulted by the violent
foreplay in the casual sex
of the American flag
blowing in the breeze,
Even the death in their
faces
Trying to give yourself to
love while playing the
slave masters, of turning
our truth into serpents and
demons that try to justify
and rationalize this state
of being alone in all of
this sensitivity sometimes
kills us.
In good fuckings, in soft
touches.
In dark and mysterious
eyes telling us they know
how it feels, while leaving
us in the morning to
contemplate their big pretty
asses and I-don't-care
attitudes walking out the
door.

Harlem dying of her own
hands at stop signs and
crack houses,
Promising the children
free rides to Coney Island
While kente cloth voices
on radios beg and plead
for handouts from bloated
poets lying in the filth
and perversion of the hope
that T.V. commercials will
pretend that we still have
imagination and creativity
sold to the highest corporate
bidder.
Past rejections and animal
urges wrapped around
triggers pulling down our
mothers,
pulling down our sisters,
pulling down our daughters
deserve more than bullets in
the head and the misery of
calling out our names in
desperation.
The death of love trying to
hold on one more time in the
drugs, in the rage, in the
bitterness of tears
streaming down your lies.
I want to win.
I want to laugh.

Brainstorms. Rainstorms. Painstorms.

Brainstorms
Rainstorms
Painstorms

The desert is full of children.
Dry mouths and parched skins.
This poem is not about demons.
It is not about magic. A tiny
drop of water upon their lips.
They ride cruise missiles
barebacked. Lollipops and jujy
fruits paced in suicide bombs.
They are dead on arrival.

The Gaza Strip.
The Sunset Strip.
The drug strip.

They are dead on arrival.
Stray bullets and boiling water
comes to grips with smothered
smile I am the voice of every
child. I am that moment when
your love becomes twisted and
you decide to construct an asylum
upon my innocence. I am that
moment when you turn off the
light and leave me struggling
and groping for imagination
becomes a pin cushion for fear
and paranoia. I am that moment
when you walk away and leave
me to my own self-devices and

live sex shows and sliding down
poles with Hershey Kisses
dripping from my mouth. The
abuse began in the womb.

Savage thrusts.
Savage thoughts.
You hated each other.

How could you love me?
And so now I run and hide
under dim streetlights exposing
our truth to the world.
Armageddon is clear. It is here.
Dead animals on the road more
and more each day.
Their blood and carcasses
propelling our progress toward
a naked sun.

I am your child.
I was your child.
I am no longer a child.

I am a threat.
I am a menace.
I am your death.

If you don't learn how to respect my touch.
Respect my feelings.
Respect my existence.

Brainstorms.
Rainstorms.
Painstorms.

New Orleans

Keep it comin, try to feel. Keep it comin and keep it real. Keep it comin and keep it true. Keep it righteous and comin to you. Don't give up, Don't give it a thought. Don't be afraid and don't get caught. Keep it comin, the young and the old. Keep it strong, courageous and bold. The music flows. Words in rhyme. Beginning to the end becomes your time. Keep your vision. Stay in sight. To be free you have to fight. One eye will shine the other stays dark. Keep it comin to keep the spark. The moment reveals. The moment embraces. Keep the smiles on our children's faces. Keep it comin. Keep it free. Reach out to the spirits across the sea. Reach out to love. Reach out to hope, Keep it comin. Reach out for the rope. My life is yours. Your life is mine. A toke of the herb. A sip of the wine. Peace to you and all you are. Keep it comin so we all can go far.

Flowing

Splendid motions in between the clouds. The stink of conspiracy fills the air. The softness of tranquility after a long hard journey.

Devious eyes open in the dark. Searching, groping, looking for ways to enslave. Trying to accept peace and the music and the lies can no longer play games of worldly proportions with small insignificant battles of bitterness and anger moving ahead on the stream of someone else's. love.

And I like being well and whole and free from self. Shoot them. Stab them. Kill them. These traits, these values, these fantasies. That have left us wallowing in the realms of Distortion.

Look at all the wildflowers smiling secretly from the cracks of their souls. Looking at life thru one-way mirrors.

Guarding their tenderness against attacks from themselves. Dark clouds on the horizon.

Understanding is being dashed against the rocks. The ripples of the sea are bringing forth blood. Where is the wind? Who has taken the wind? I can't breathe this foul air. An air that reeks with the stench of death.

We turn to the water.

Old slaves seeking a new freedom, one little touch of kindness can become warm hugs and love and prayers for the dead and their living dreams sound so real in the echoes of pain and laughter on the faces of children.

The need in you speaks to the need in me. I hear a harmony in your voice.

A harmony I haven't heard before then realize the closeness of your touch has just been a few sincere words away begin to feel strong and at ease watching you watch the water I am growing. I'm getting better. The struggle has not been in vain.

For the first time in my life I don't need the unnecessary to make me feel like a man in your presence slowly takes me out to get on gentle waves of confidence.

Rhythmagic

Rhythmagic, the music of the word.
Now you hear it, now you don't.
Now you feel it, now you won't.
The thought of pure genius against
all odds and trying to love our
children in fast lanes and subway
cars. Tenderness in between the stops.
They smile and touch our faces.
The lyrics. The songs.

The beat of death is so painful in the rejection of

Your soul, my soul all wanting to
believe in that touch. To believe
it will always be there. To keep
it healing. To keep it safe, to keep
it warm in the midst of cold and
lifeless expressions. Too sensitive.
Too afraid. Too human.

And the cold-blooded murder of imagination in women's
flesh and blood of true lovers depending on full moons
right minds.

Listen, can't you hear the naked
mornings in the raindrops on the
window pane as the high leaves you.
Rhythmagic. The music of the word.
Now you hear it, now you don't.
Now you feel it, now you won't.

love's promise to come see us tomorrow.

eyes blinded by sounds of trust and the
and the sanity of mad musicians in their

Wilt

When the flowers have smiled their last smile and handshakes and congratulations hold on to one more dance in the corners of empty champagne bottles and loneliness catches the bridal bouquet in the middle of thoughts and doubts when I lay my body down next to yours exhausted from the fear of losing something very special to strangers and friends all at the same time will tell if this is who we really are in the drama of coming attractions when we find it so hard to express our feelings will you then marry me in that moment of memories, pictures and happiness, when I forgot to ask you to please remember that I am only human.

When worldly affairs and your touch make me want to run and hide in winter storms and temptation and lust lie to love on silk sheets of denial and rejection begging and pleading for your eyes to meet mine for some soft apology over impromptu lunches and long walks into empty arms and promising careers of pretending to be happy by the fire and pain holding up very well considering the fact that I find myself alone in the thought of some ridiculous smile and half empty glass and bar stools and wondering why I can't humble myself to unconditional love and poems and prayers asking you to please remember that I am only human.

When I have found my way back to change and the courage to be a friend in your eyes will speak to me of the beauty of sacrifice and the humility of serving time waiting on one of us to be true to the words we spoke in the music, in the laughter, in the dancing on thin ice of wondering if you still care for me in this indecision of feelings and reason and dreams binding me to be there for you through all the confusion and hesitation of just wanting to let it be me for you in that moment when I close your eyes or you close mine, please remember that I always loved you.

Asian Winds

Going east trying to find a smoother ride. Asian clouds rolling up under the plane kissing me tender in my thoughts. My mind too is of that intelligence of living in the world and keeping it safe and real for beauty is in the eyes of the beholder of love and patience.

We must be patient with those who have not learned the lessons of truth and giving to the vision is now! The new world is now! A closed society full of open hearts. The waters in the fountains. The poetry is what you feel and love for the colors of the garden and Japanese parks in the exotic smell of flowers and black birds singing morning songs to shrines.

So alone and together are man and nature in this struggle to preserve the culture of peace and serenity the mind spilling outwards overflowing with sincerity and truth. I see God in you, in my eyes, in our pain, in our confusion and doubts. He is speaking to us in prayers, in chants, in the loneliness of just trying to be human as possible.

The language of women in silence and subtle images wrapping themselves around your imagination and senses roaming the streets and geisha houses in newfound freedom lost in the ways of the old. The incense burning into the heavens of past glory and radioactive tears falling from Mt. Fuji. The spirit is the thing! The spirit is the thing.

The passion of the ancestors is in the sun. See their faces. The kindness of the ancestors is in the moon. See their faces, the strength of the ancestors is in the ocean. See their faces, the determination of the ancestors is in tomorrow. See their faces.

Sonny

The family left Alabama only to leave you open to the cold northern winds. The genius of your walk. The hipness of your sadness. Tight stingy brim hunkered down on a head full of thick and wooly hair. You were Afrocentric before its time. You did not like Tarzan. The Fourth of July and educated negroes.

You could be brilliant at times from the muted sound of your trumpet to the muted sound of your soul to the muted sound of your tears falling upon the wrong town, the wrong time, the wrong family. You were special, Daddy, the style and grace you initiated when you decided to direct that trumpet towards your lips while gently fingering the keys your eyes focused on that point of the forth coming sound.

I heard your interpretations of the sickness, distortion, and beauty of our past. I heard your interpretations of the sickness, distortion, and beauty of our family. A classic duo that could have been but never was. Somehow your phrasing and my tone always seemed to get in the way. That insurgent harmony that kept us clashing and crashing into one another.

That very strident sound of the misappropriation of very wanting and needing melodies. There was love for you here, Daddy. There was love for you here. All day Saturdays on Howard Street I was hustling for us, for you and some money in your pocket. For you and a pack of cigarettes. For you and your dignity and just a little more time.

I used to sit on the basement steps and
marvel at the fluid motion of your pen upon
paper. You made it look so easy. The G clefs.
The notes. The chords. The lines. The bridges.
The spacing. All those musical symbols and
indentations.

With all the complexities of a musician's
mind and the passion of a poet, you sometimes
lingered, casually strolled on the very
delicate and outer fringes of madness. I was
on your side. 1 was waiting on you. I was
listening anxiously for that new sound, that
new direction,

that new form that could keep me focused and
in the presence of pyramids, temples, and
civilizations rose and fell on the strength
and imagination of our dreams, ideas, and
notes. Falling in line on time. That three-
quarter note. That half note. That sixteenth
note. That flatted fifth. That blue note.

That very very blue note and 40 ounces in
the dark corners of juke joints and
honkytonks of feeling good in the picking
and strumming of country banjoes and that
32nd note moving faster than the speed of
Satchmo and Miles and you in the motion in
the jamming in the forests in the woods

in those moments of rapture moving forward in the heat and humid questions of, is that your daddy? Is that your daddy playing that horn? I began to chase the darkness in the light of your absence. My sense of you made no since at all.

And so the question remained who were you and what did you mean to me. And then one day, by the grace of God, I came face to face with you again in aneurism on a respirator. Your lonely and sullen eyes kindly pleading. Let your daddy go, son. Tell them to let your daddy go.

And I did. I closed your eyes as I would have closed the last pages of a magnificent novel. I gently set your ashes out to sea. To keep your spirit clean. To keep your spirit near. I forgive you, Daddy. I forgive you. Because I have learned how to forgive myself. Peace be still.

The Queen Mothers

Scattered remnants on Robben Island.
Scattered remnants on Rikers Island.
Scattered remnants on Caribbean Islands.
Scattered remnants on South American Islands.
There are footprints in Mexico
and Central America also.
Somewhere behind some African hill there is a
glorious past that was tortured, maligned,
and ground into the dust.

A feminine voice cries out:
Where are my princes?
Where are my visionaries?
Where are my philosophers,
my poets, my warriors,
my kings, my protection?

She walks at a fast pace
with a slight limp.
She is poor.
She is single.
She is a work in progress,
so far from perfection and
yet so close to beauty.

The drugs and the alcohol
have tried to numb her,
dumb her, succumb her
to all things that matter,
to all things considered.

The laughter of the wind
tells me she is sad.
To love is just
a moment away.
But time has no realness,
no conception of her needs.

Reaching out in a moment
of impatience is when she
feels like a poem half-written,
half-remembered,
stuck somewhere
between the warmth of sensitivity
and the blunt edge of death.

What is it about
these voluminous doe eyes,
soft warm smiles, and
magnificent physical structures
that aroused such a curiosity
and depravity to descend upon us
like crazed baboons?

Ma Rainey sang about it.
Bessie Smith sang about it.
Ella Fitzgerald sang about it.
Sarah Vaughn sang about it.
Nancy and Aretha sang about it.
What happened to my crown?
Why has my glory been dismissed?
When will my respect return?

...the Queen Mothers

She takes anything for everything and
everything for nothing at all. On her
knees, on her feet, on her back, and
even on her good days she is a target
for abuse, neglect, and disappointment.
But somewhere between that first sex
and last lie she decides to make a change.

She climbs into her space.
Her soul is on fire.
She wants to know the truth,
speak the truth,
and live the truth!
She decided to make the journey on her
own.

They are leaving us behind.
They are taking the game back,
making up their own rules as they go
along.
We can't fool them anymore.
We never could, really.
They are connecting to their ancestors to
their inspirations past and present.

And there are many:
Queen Candace absolute ruler and
commander
of her army that stopped Alexander the
Great in his tracks at the borderline of
the first cataract.

Queen Nzinga who taught the
Portuguese a few tricks of her
own.
Cleopatra who had all those Roman
boys going in and out of their
minds.
Queen Nefertari of the Great
Eighteenth Dynasty.
Queen Hatshepsut the greatest
pharaoh of all of Egypt.
Queen Mother Moore, queen of our
diaspora and Queen of Harlem.

Phyllis Wheatley a great American
Poet.
Harriet Tubman who not only freed
slaves but got them how to free
their minds also.
Septima Clark who taught black
men and women how to read and
write so they could register to
vote in Mississippi.

Mary McCloud Bethune, educator.
Ella Baker who taught boys how to
become men and men how to become
revolutionaries.
Fanny Lou Hamel who showed the
world her courage, strength and
determination in her struggle for
democracy.
Shirley Chisholm, first Black
Woman candidate for President of
The United States of America.

Barbara Jordan, politician of high
moral character,
master orator and debater.
And Maya Angelou who knew why the
caged bird sang because she was such
a phenomenal woman
as was
Lizzie Walker
Margaret Ponder Blakely
Rose Fuller and Barbara Jean Fuller
all grand special and unique women.

And they rise. And they rise. And they rise.

The Queen Mothers

Kings of Pain

Kings of Africa in the kings of Spain
The king of demons in the kings of pain

Up the low-rider down in the seat
Driving by while pumping the beat

Innocent bystanders all in a row
The white ones in drag, the black ones don't know

Prime examples of the primal need
Cries for acceptance become cries of greed

To the best of darkness they give their regard Making hard so easy, easy so hard

Heroes born to dead statistics
Forensic medicine and police ballistics

They only talk when it's time to cry
They only live when it's time to die

Famous fathers and famous sons
Famous massacres with famous guns

From stickup kid to be
From a trying birth to just trying to be

The sorrow in the color of daddy's eyes
Living in the pain of daddy's lies

Holding his memory, holding his hand
Holding the gun that stole his land

Shooting up corners, shooting up dreams
Shooting up veins in unconscious streams

Addicted to using, addicted to recovery
Addicted to self-deception at the expense of self-discovery

Stingy affections from a stingy brim
The pain gets brighter as the streetlights dim

The drama, the marks, the gators, the skins
Players who become chumps to players' grins

Navy SEALS with Navy crosses
Cutting throats to cut their losses

Legitimate killers cool and glow
Waiting to exhale while waiting to go

Funny little sounds filling up space
Round about midnight changes pace

Loving mothers become abused wives
Molested daughters become bitches with knives

Domestic violence becomes foreign affairs
Delayed stress playing musical chairs

Poison darts and poison gag
Poisoned touches at Catholic Mass

Afraid to let God, afraid to let go
Afraid to commit and learn to grow

Dirty little secrets in dirty little places
Empty frustrations in full clown faces

Afraid to be humble, afraid to be wise
Afraid of the truth in some woman's eyes

Politicians and lobbyists in smoke-filled rooms
Consigning the masses to terror-filled tombs

To save the children to erase their fears
To hold them close and kiss their tears

Drug dealers and skinheads in the morning news United
in the state of dysfunctional blues

From the highly principled to the highly insane
America is home to the Kings of Pain!

Young Love

Another young man died yesterday. His bloodstained presence slammed against our sunrises. How and when will we begin to cherish the welcome of his smile.

A man-child submerged in the purple liquid of night. They fall aimlessly thru the cracks of darkness. The full moon becomes a partner, a silent partner in shutting down bars. Shutting down cities. Shutting down dreams of Daddy walking and talking while holding your hand.

Our children cry out to us from their fears, from their suicides, from their innocence and loneliness being betrayed by lazy pimps and limp smiles.

The opera is in full form. The drama unfolds. The violin is both tragic and comforting. The piano, light and inspiring. The crescendos between light and darkness are truly stunning.

This could have been a true love story full of twists and turns of pain and triumph of the game begins to evolve from shine shines to stickups from stickups to B and E from B an E to quiet hustles from quiet hustles to residing in that comfort zone between high crimes and misdemeanors.

New songs from old radios where crippled poems lounge in digital wheelchairs whistling in the dark while spitting acrobatic words at boombox musicians who scratch and sample the wax from the devil's ears while conducting bling bling concertos that howl at the moon.

In all those projects. In all those quick glimpses of death. In all those sudden and unwanted intrusions lurking inside your paranoia begins to open wide to receive your transition from champagne and free base to crack and Olde English just like that.

Where is the glory? What was the glamour? Who were the police? What happened in the shootouts? Why were so many bullets left in the wind? In the walls, in the chests of 23-year-old young men standing In the wrong places at the wrong time.

Their last breath of manhood simply pleading: Don't let me die. Don't let me die. Please, don't let me die.

MEN-tality!

Easy little toke. Easy little rush. Some easy illusion to soften the crush. The inner soul. The outer glee. Exciting moments that beg to be free. Don't worry, I've got control. That lurking madness in my soul. My soul. Precise. Intense. So focused on goal. Truth becomes pretense. The lie becomes bold.

The morning is need. The night satisfaction. Moments become open to fatal attraction. Pretty little girls in pretty little sighs. Pretty little deceptions become pretty little highs. The movie. The song. The opening scene. Moments that sparkle and then become so mean. Slow dance. Fast dance. Fast forward into reverse. The imagination becomes doubtful. And then a curse.

Nanoseconds. Mainframes. And cybernetics. Hackers. Mavericks. And mental prosthetics. Digital clones on digital screens. Accepting progress and then accepting fiends. Vampire cultures. Garlic and blood. Standing on principles while standing in mud.

So casual. So social. So pervasive the use. What's good for the gander becomes deadly to the goose. The beginning. The middle. The end becomes question. Morals are closed but open to suggestion. Shady positions without shade in the trees. Major destruction in minor degrees.

Demons begin to make their call. The mighty cathedrals begin to fall. Constitutional crisis and voter projections. Your vote is important but not in elections. Into the Prozac. Into the pool. Into the process of becoming a fool. Bright shiny Negroes take their places. Wide open smiles on tight little faces. With political savvy and degrees in hand. Shedding their skins while surveying the land.

Besides themselves beside their master. Forty acres, a mule, and a ghetto blaster. Systems flashing! Systems down! The virtual reality of a night on the town. Trojan horses that can't be rode. Well-strapped cowboys that can't be throwed.

Slowly the days become indecision. Slowly the fear loses the vision. The seconds, the minutes, and then the hours. Dreams become insults and then wilting flowers. The rumors keep you living. Your last sense of pride. Partially hopeful. And then partially denied. Lonely women and fireplaces. Burning memories into their faces. Roaches in corners. And women in bars. The beauty becomes ugly and lost in the stars.

Empty bottles against the wall. A knock on the door. A sound in the hall. Kiss me long. Kiss me now. Tell me you love me, but don't tell me how. You cross my mind and I don't know why. Sometimes your spirit makes my body cry. Public insanity in mirrors and smoke. Sincerely yours in the name of coke!

Hip hop. Can't stop the drop. Who is getting paid? The game is playing with fire while players are getting played. Highly mediocre becomes highly paid. Highly empowered and then highly afraid. To shake that shadow. To take that stroll. To let the mind take its toll.

Life or death which way to go. One more denial becomes one more blow. Can't see the forest. Can't see the trees. Can't feel the change in the coming breeze. God becomes distant and yet so close. Easy comes and then easy goes. Caught in between the coming back. Caught in the moment of the closing act. What to lose. What to find. A positive frame in a state of mind.

Waking up the morning to the beginning of you. Waking up to be sure to see it through. The circle begins where the circle ends. Back in the mix of family and friends. So what's the puzzle? What's the quiz? Enjoy the moment, that's all there is. So, here's to the thought. Here's to the mind. Here's to that moment we all must find.

Jimi Ju Ju

An easy sunrise precedes a touch of madness. Touching the miracles. Touching the sleep. Lingering lyrics falling graciously upon water-filled eyelids. Foot pedal and sly smile all moving in the same direction, the same motion, the same rhythm of Congo Square and primitive string instruments defying the burdens of slavery.

Little Richard and Otis Reading. Sam Cooke and James Brown all saw and felt the passion of this genius of rare humility trying to get out to sea. The laughter of idiots bleeting in his ears. The mother Nile pleases in more ways than one. The music in his stride has put his demons to sleep, he hopes. A white mist encircles the innocence of his Harlem baptism.

The Village calls. London beckons. So kind. So warm. So devouring. Ju Ju Jimi. Jimi. Jimi. Ju Ju Ju Ju Jimi. Ju Ju Ju Ju Jimi Ju Ju. Yes! He was the Voo Doo Child. This is where he lived, this is where he thrived. In the frayed and fragile wires connected to dangling dimly lit neon signs unconsciously flickering one last tribute to Miles Davis solo over rain-drenched vomit from the bowels of broken promises and dreams deferred.

He kept turning on the rhythm and blues. They kept trying to turn it off. The loneliness of trusted friends dropping your name carelessly upon the wind. Staring in the reflections of Jimi God. Jimi Prophet. Jimi visionary of pointless sights. Pointless reasons. Pointless memories. Teetering and rotting Roman columns peeking through lively magnolia trees whispering Charlie Patton.

Son House and the spirit of Robert Johnson and his serpentine wailing of the Mississippi blues bent over sun-scorched morning abandoned by God and devil inside your mind. Your sound. Your music creating artforms faster than the speed of deceit. Where is the deception Jimi? What does it look like? What land does it frequent? What fragrance does it indulge in? What flower does it wear in its lapel? Where is the deception Jimi?

Ooooh can you see. By the dawn's early light. And the rocket's red glare. The bombs bursting in air. And the machine - guns Jimi. And the machine - guns Jimi. And the machine - guns Jimi. And the guns. And the guns. And the guns. And the violence of charred and burning flesh of children amusing themselves in the shadows of drunken and addicted stupors you climb stairs to find yourself in the despair.

No more lust! No more lust! No more lurid decisions and business contracts in the thrusts of darkened rooms and phony orgasms of pretending to be you - are the Foxy Lady and I am the Wild Thing - will you please take your loneliness out of me - I'm tired of playing this game. He kept turning on the rhythm and blues. They kept trying to turn it off.

One night I danced with the real Atlanta in a juke joint on the Northside. My Hennessey took her Red Bull to new heights in the music of the saints and to a band of gypsies. There is a dance that the poet dances. In the eyes. In the eyes of demons. In the eyes of children soothe his soul with kind gestures and beaming smiles they release their dreams to his word.

They trust his jagged edges and sharp turns into funeral dirges and poetry slams for control freaks on the other side of pop culture there is a disease that festers on the pitter patter of busy feet of drug boys running through their night visions and day dreams bedazzled by slight of hands scribbling on jail house walls in small letters and close encounters with death and their illusions of power being reduced to its most common denominator.

Where is the deception Jimi? What does it look like? What land does it frequent? What fragrance does it indulge in? What flower does it wear in its lapel? Where is the deception Jimi? No Jimi. No. Don't look back. Don't look back, Jimi. Be careful. Watchout! Watchout! Don't Jimi! Don't Jimi! Don't look back. No. No No. Keep going forward. Don't look back. Please, don't look back No Jimi. No Jimi. No, no.

It's too late Here comes that, second glance. Here comes that act of denial. And the guitars on fire. And the static from the Electric Lady. No Jimi. Don't look back. Here comes their entourages of schizophrenia. Here comes their anxieties. Here comes their depression. Their heavy-handed Baroque counterpoints. And the fingers crisscrossing, freefalling, and tiptoeing between the forces of good and evil.

Ju Ju Ju Ju. Jimi. Jimi. Ju Ju. Back to the forest Jimi. Back to the forest. Ju Ju. Jimi. Jimi. Ju Ju Ju Ju. Back to where the Twin Rivers meet. Ju Ju. Jimi. Jimi. Jimi Jimi. Ju Ju. Back to the healing. Jimi Jimi. Ju Ju Ju Ju. Back to the way Jimi. Back to the way. Our way. Ju Ju Ju Ju. JIMI JIMI JIMI. Ju Ju Ju Ju Ju ju Jimi. ARE YOU EXPERIENCED JIMI? ARE YOU EXPERIENCED JIMI? ARE YOU EXPERIENCED!

Purple haze are in my brain.
Losing self to lose this pain.
Embracing the truth and wanting to fly.
'Scuse me beauty while I kiss your sky!

Homesick

The screams
The land screaming
Women and children screaming
Men's dignity and respect screaming.
The screams inside that separate the emotions pushing
us over the edge into self-hatred and contempt for the
success and happiness of big chiefs, little chiefs.
Large tribes. Small tribes. The ancestors all connected
by chains linked to their past insecurities and future
deja vu.

Your mother
was once my mother.
My father was once your father.
My house was your house to the rest of the storm.
In the war, in the luxurious and extravagant
whorehouses of Western philosophy that apprehends our
mother's and sister's smile.

In only
this God we trust.
The one that consumes
our very manhood in the bastard and illegitimate ideas
wrapped up in some green and putrid religion. Time is
money. Money is time. Down to the docks. Packed in.
Beat in. Thrown in. Even the ships have no mercy, they
speak to us of coming evils, subtle pleasures and open
decadence.

General Motors
and the Pillsbury Doughboy.
You will become the sleazy
and slimy characters in someone else's mind.
You will become the kindness that is truly a weakness.
The ocean hears this assault upon our being. It becomes
our friend. It shows compassion. Jump! Jump! Come to
me. The waters become a deep and dark red. The sharks
feast on our desire to be free. Bodies flowing in their
own thoughts. Children clinging to dead mothers. The
inevitability of death smashing them in the face. Men
searching the waters for families. Families searching
the water for one last memory. The African shore
dying in their final grasp for air. Tears now become
dreams in a world of standing still. Torn and broken
bodies paint the horizon with a terror that betrays
the very essence of God.

The blood.
All that blood.
How can we forget?
A seat in the audience of the Grammy Awards.
How can we forget? A new anchor job telling
respectable lies. How can we forget? Your hopes
wrapped around some depraved manner. We arrive. The
new rhythm is waiting, so are they. The new rhythm is
demanding, so are they. They shuffle and smile in the
glint and glimmer of the western sun. Very private and
secret war dances as he sneaks in on the wind. A
charming addiction seeking warmth His presence
precedes him. The perversion is so unique.

The lust so warm.
So kind. She begins
to get into the rhythm.
I suffocate my rage. I was my anger in the light of
the Moon. I have to believe that things will get better
in this darkness of over-exaggerated grunts and moans.
The children leave the circle, eyes rolling back into
their heads. Their truths in a coma. Beside vigils and
Jay McShann. Yes! The creativity is still there.
Somebody has to do this for humanity. Moving right
along. We take the bombings. We take the lynchings. We
take the rapes. And we smile. And we sing. And we
dance. And we love. We love thru all the reefer smoke.
Thru all the slow jams and hot numbers and dream
books and poor black women dancing with their welfare
checks in subsidized dreams and empty cognac bottles
pretending to be romance and warm hugs and tears on
the verge of denying the children the future for a
chance to enjoy and experience the true meaning of
just one loving kiss.

Bench warrants
snatch away the freedom
of hands on bars hoping the criminal justice
system won't plea bargain away your imagination while
speaking in dead tongues and handcuffed to the mercy
of dollar signs and the hollow words of, get out of the
car, you're under arrest. Take that word "insane" and
make it "warrior." Take that word "crazy" and make it
"poet." Take that word "suicidal" and make it live in
some kind and loving expression for those who cannot
raise their heads above the shrieks and shrills of the
sirens and automatic weapons.

We owe no explanations.
We owe no apologies.
Ours has been a struggle of gun battles
and bullets whizzing past our sensitivity and
arrogance all mixed up in alcohol and drugs. Climb out
of your bottles Climb out of your clouds and vapors.
Climb out of the centuries of being less than the
thought you really wanted to share. Grow into the
journey. The sun breaking thru the clouds. The
simplicity and beauty of good morning your smile and
touch. We used to feel these things. We used to be
sacred to each other's thoughts and expressions. We
were true artists. Not afraid of giving too much too
soon and looking too foolish. We were there at the
beginning of faith and trust and respect behind closed
doors we used to speak to each other in the soft tones
of the rainbow smiling thru the river's mist cooling
the warmth and passion of time waiting for us to come
home.

Sort it out

The dreams that we stalk or the dreams that stalk us lose their passion, their fire on the tongues of rumor or whatever others may think of us. We become casualties of war before the war has begun. We lie down and surrender to the slightest thought that someone else may possess something that we can't find within ourselves. I am a Poet! What do you want from me? Guilt. Remorse. Name. Rank and serial number. How much more of a companion and peasant must I be? There is no sin that you can give me that I haven't already given to myself. From Niggerdom to Martyrdom I am strapped with poetic explosives. I only seek your minds and your acceptance of who you really are. You cannot hide your humanity. You cannot disguise it. You cannot put it in a closet, close the door and walk away from it. It will break free and it will find you and leave you stranded in confusion and wanting. Denial and defiance is a lot of work. The excuses. The exaggerations. The flashlight in the dark seeking out your shadow's name. The mirrors are fearless. They throw back the blood and the false images. There are children in the streets who have been spawned, by their mother's pain. By their father's pain. By the pornography of America's masturbation and orgasms of anal retentive oral dissertations in the very high academic places searching for answers in the cool and calm of street smarts. Why do we become different people at the same time in the wrong places? Call up your demons. Call up your jinn. Let them go. Let them run side by side

with the angels. The light side and the dark side trying to find some change in the depths of your pockets or the shallowness of your minds. Sort it out in the exhaustion of prayers on three-day binges and one-night stands. Let the moment take you to the edge and then stop! Look down and look up. And then look back. And smile. And be patient. Hear the music. Find someone to dance with. Hold them sincerely and gently. And learn.
To be content.
To be content.
To be content.

25 Years

The innocence of youth and age
betrayed by the times we used

                to dream of being men in movies
            and lies destroyed by our own

passion for the truth. The same
smiles and humor so sensitive

                to being cared for and loved by
              those who say they understand.

This is no easy thing being the
strength for the weakness and

                fear of words lost in the dreams
              and nights of Harlem our

inspiration to leave and come
back to in times of madness and

                coke and jail. We love each other
              in the contempt for ourselves

and what we have to do. No one
has said it or done it better

                than us, you, me, we are the last
              hope for those who cringe in the

corners of themselves and believe
that there is no way out of the

                projects and bitterness of flirting
                with the edge and beautiful women

and moments of peace and substance
abuse and the frustration of being

                    too good, too soon, too early. Only
                      we know what we have seen. Only

we know what we have felt. Only
we know what we have shared at the

                    expense of being the warriors and
                      lovers of the self—hatred and

death that charm our hopes
with cheap tricks of

                    rehabilitation of promises too
                    addicted to losing and quitting

the game of being human and
private confessions of just

                    wanting to be who we are. We
                    are the friends to the tears

that have nowhere to go. We
are our fathers in that moment

                    of night that speaks only to
                    the softness of compassion. We

are the doubt and hesitation on
corners in bars and in love with

                    our people and being so much a
                    part of their pain and laughter

we sacrifice ourselves to the
neon lights and being close to

                    one another in the morning will
                    come only when we learn how to

control the darkness of ourselves.

Monument

The **corner,** a simple place. Pure words. Pure game. Pure entertainment. A dirty crumpled shirt over here. A Wild Irish Rose bottle over there. A high-heel sneaker delicately balancing itself on the curb of the **corner** of your smile, in the **corner** of our dreams. Young love with school books in their hands lean on the mailbox that leans on the **corner** that leans in the direction of the Temptations and Dells doo-wopping on the **corner** of Woodward Ave. and 47th Street. We congregated. We overstated. We underrated. We educated.

The **corner** was our time when time stood still in gators and snakeskins in yellow and pink and powder blue profiles glorifying their 15 minutes of fame. The **corner** caressed our Robitussin smiles and glazed eyes. It was Bebop and Hip Hop all at the same time. It nurtured our sense of expression, our flair for the dramatic like choosing fees. Shots being fired. Outlaw ho's wife in-laws. Police brutality. Bottom women. Guns to the head. And pimpin sho ain't easy. The **corner** was our magic, our music, our politics. Fires raged as tribal dances and war cries broke out on different **corners.** Power to the people. Black power. Black is beautiful. But the **corner** stood strong.

It gave voice to our frustrations and anxieties. It became platforms for our messengers and prophets. The **corner** was our Rock of Gibraltar. Our Stonehenge. Our Taj Mahal. Our monument. Our testimonial to freedom, to peace and to love down on the **corner.**

HOLLOW WOOD

Fragile warriors
on suicide missions
into the feminine
and masculine
interpretations of
soft words following
the wind into
the pain
of denying yourself to live
in the beauty of
street women
touching your eyes with vision
into being at ease with the craft of human drama.
Every day, every hour, every moment
on public display
for those who are afraid
to be real in the streets,
In your God,
in your selfish reasons
to play games with childhood fantasies
bordering on the verge of
cute baby pictures
and hard-core pornography
left to the mercy of cocaine intrusions
into corporate frustrations and welfare checks
fumbling around in the dark of
Africa misplaced by well-meaning
missionary positions in
crack hotels full of American dreams
going up in smoke.
Pretending heavily on the sanity and reason
of snow queens and captains of industry
dancing to the new rock band

and the crucifix curled up in the smiles
of hoochie mamas
standing on corners admiring the coolest
and newly released jailhouse walk.
He missed her in the first squint
of her homeless eyes
searching the sad and tragic remains
of something that once was real
hiding behind the facade of good breeding and good cigars
listening to the recycled chamber music while
masturbating on the telephone numbers
of young and nubile virgins.
Mr. DeMille, I'm ready for my closeup now!

Grace

Eyes oven in the womb. The struggle arrives to turn darkness into light. Dangling on the wines of the Phoenix. The creative process begins to turn ugly. Vandalizing and robbing graves of child prodigies turning into serious discussion of mass murder and the therapeutic value of Saturday morning shopping sprees.

That ancient rage has found the fountain of youth. The betrayal of genius is burning at the stake. The spider descends. The violence is always there. The web embraces us all. More insidious than drugs. More pleasurable than sex. Slightly entangled. Slightly confused.

That possible criminal element awakens you to the terror and loneliness of running and screaming into the silent pain of someone else looking to you for answers. Ours was a moment so divine and yet so very unholy all around us danced morning prayers giving praises to the lord of the universe while we became atheistic to the thought of giving love to one another.

Glamorous and well-financed pools of blood profiling on neighborhood corners while smiling at and tempting the boldest gangster rap. Ours had become a comedy of error. A tragedy from the dark side of the moon. Conversations had become shrieks and shrills in the echoes of laughter. But still we tried two muted poets cemented together by the glamour of ticker-tape parades.

Had we become petrified artists who could only paint terrified portraits of love. Had we lost inspiration in the dark and slimy swamps of some foreign smile. The wealth we squandered on poor excuses and starving lines of poetry inspired by the tenderness of your smile healed me, cleansed me, of my indifference to the Holy Scriptures should have told us something about trying to be children of God.

in all of this madness against all these odds of being too intense and too delicate to be real lovers in real time. Run run run to the birth to harmony so wise and peaceful desires to go back to the beginning to be good to yourself and others are searching too.

Sacred to the Pain

Mama holding my hand in the storm. Audience participation heavy in my dreams. The church choir is singing my favorite inspiration. God is alive. God is real. He is alive right here in my hands. He is on gigs in funky Midwestern clubs. Roll with us baby. Roll with us. Shower us with that funk. That country funk. Backwoods, swamp, and bayou funk. Way back into the bottom of slave ships. And deep dark funky screams that caress our souls and make us pat our feet to the rhythm, to the blues to the jazz and to the music in your heart makes us want to dance.

And so I play. Walking thru their smiles. Pain up tempo. Sensitivity opened to the four winds. I want you to feel this thing I feel when finger touches strings. This strange thing that kisses my lips. Whispers in my ears. Embraces all that I am. This thing called love. Love with no one to receive it. Love with no one to understand it. Love with no one to care for it. Musical discontent. Eyes rolling back in my head. Need something. No not that. My head needs something. No not that. Temporary pleasure becomes permanent emotions that separate leaving me in so many places. Musical genius. Musical demon. So fragile. So vulnerable. So very real to myself.

All I've got is your appreciation. Please listen. It is so lonely. So very lonely down here in all of this sound all of this passion forcing itself upon my reason. This is for you, Mama. This is for you. For all the worry. For all of the tears wasted on worthless days. For all the time that I've climbed into my fears without praying. For all the bitterness and rage you've turned into magic and beauty.

And now I lay me down to sleep. And I pray my soul the music will keep. Up to the bridge. I hear the chord. On my way to meet my Lord. I leave you my soul. I leave you my heart. One more solo before I depart. The church choir is singing my favorite inspiration. God is real. God is alive. He is right here in my hands. Listen.

Love

Loving kisses and loving sighs. To have love's pleasure bring tears to my eyes. Love at first sight is so very rare. Love may come late but it always comes fair. Tears that humble. Tears that smile. Tears that comfort and then beguile. Where are the drugs? Where is the sex? Where is the pleasure when there's nothing next? Some love to love. Some love to hate. Some find love but then it's too late. Games and lies where love should be. Someone does it to you and then you do it to me. Perversions, distortions inside the head. When illusion dictates love is dead. Love is not paranoia, love is not insecure. When a man becomes a friend is when a woman becomes sure. Love is the touch of a woman's hand, the respect for that touch is what makes a man. The thought of love on its way to you. The anticipation of what to do.

That funny little feeling that comes inside. Emotions run wild but then try to hide. Is he coming or is she not? Affection needs tenderness and they both need a lot. Why is it so hard to be at ease? Why can't I be humble and just try to please. Selfish desires that lead into doubt. Sacrifice brings joy but love brings you out. Soft morning clouds rush to cover the moon, like an orgasm with a future that comes too soon. So when the thought of quitting begins to lose your mind, put love before pain and leave the sorrow behind.

One night I was truly seeking, I was standing inside the rain. As love passed by it whispered, time to leave the pain. I'm here whenever you need me, I am the beckoning call. I can be your rise to glory or the madness before the fall. I cried out, Love what do you want from me? You've got to tell me now. Love just smiled and answered, must I also tell you how. To find that love again, the love you needed most. The only friend you had when everyone was playing ghost.

Two star-crossed lovers caught up in that infamous strain. Love becomes the struggle that tries to keep them sane. In the glorious midst of nature, they try reaching out one night. She learns how to kiss the darkness, he learns how to set his sight. Love becomes: the morning that shine so radiant and bright, it becomes the hope and promise that once was a lonely night. Where is that true beginning? Where has it all gone? Why has love become a memory that just sadly lingers on?

Hard laughter disguising softer fears. Love becomes entangled while deception cheers. Love that moment you can't understand. It's when love is asking for a helping hand. Intelligence is vital, love takes reason. Passion without wisdom is romantic treason. Love is the rain that greens the leaves, it's the part of death that never grieves. The love of money can become the love of greed. The love of denial can become the love of need. Love is a woman so deep in thought. A moment so precious it can't be bought.

That first kiss will always remain the same, if not in principle at least in name. Love is exciting. Love is bold. Love grows gracefully but never grows old. Love is being alone but never lonely. It's yours truly and yours only. It's when you think you should but know you won't. It's when they think you're convinced but then you don't. Love plus patience can become understanding. When love becomes too promiscuous it becomes too de3manding. Waiting on love can become the love of time. Being patient with love can lead to serious crime.

Love is top be considerate. Love is to be kind. It's a wise old gesture from a childish mind. To never take advantage. To never accuse. To never mistrust. To never abuse. Love is to be honored. Love is to be shared. Love is to be tried, but never dared. Love is to be desire. Love is to yearn. To be able to give and ask for nothing in return. And to be able to speak so true, I love you. And I love you, too.

Power

Power is definitely in the eyes of the beholder. The vanity embraces chaos as the pride becomes bolder and day by day as usual and slowly by the hour, the beholder begins to lose its humanity and then definitely its power...

© Copyright
3/8/14

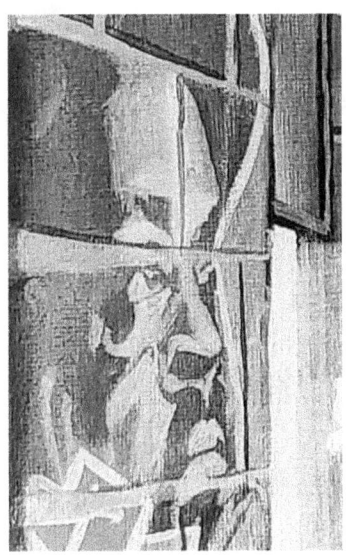

An Ohio native, Umar Bin Hassan sold his younger sister's record player to purchase a bus ticket to New York City. It was there that he joined the Last Poets, the prototype rappers born of the Civil Rights Era, "who used obstreperous verse to chide a nation whose inclination was to maintain the colonial yoke around the neck of the disenfranchised." (https://www.globaldarkness.com/articles/last_poets_biography.htm)

In 1993, Umar released his first solo album, *Be Bop or Be Dead* (Axiom Records). He's also released *To the Last* (Baraka Foundation, 2001) and *Life Is Good* (Stay Focused Records, 2002).

From international festivals to public parks to Saturday Night Live he's been on numerous stages while picking up Grammy wins along the way. Umar hasn't slowed down at all, as he still travels the globe delivering memorable performances.

When he feels like resting, he does so in Baltimore, Maryland.

www.ingramcontent.com/pod-product-compliance
Lightning Source LLC
Chambersburg PA
CBHW050656160426
43194CB00010B/1964